HAL•LEONARD®
GUITAR
PLAY-ALONG

AUDIO
ACCESS
INCLUDED

PLAYBACK+
Speed • Pitch • Balance • Loop

Acoustic

T0058904

2	**Angie** THE ROLLING STONES
8	**Behind Blue Eyes** THE WHO
14	**Best of My Love** THE EAGLES
20	**Blackbird** THE BEATLES
25	**Dust in the Wind** KANSAS
30	**Layla** ERIC CLAPTON
37	**Night Moves** Bob Seger
46	**Yesterday** THE BEATLES

Tracking, mixing, and mastering by Jake Johnson
All guitars by Doug Boduch
Bass by Tom McGirr
Keyboards by Warren Wiegratz
Drums by Scott Schroedl

ISBN 0-634-05623-9

To access audio visit:
www.halleonard.com/mylibrary

5814-8277-0750-6383

Visit Hal Leonard Online at www.halleonard.com

This book not for sale in the E.U.

HAL•LEONARD®

Angie

Words and Music by Mick Jagger and Keith Richards

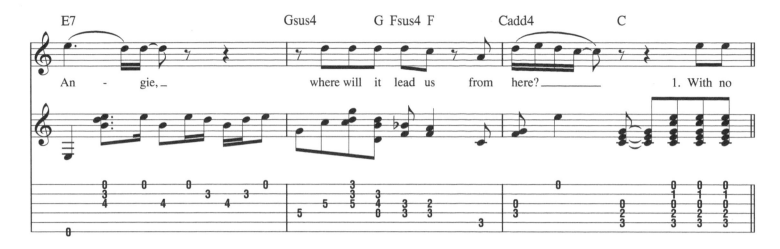

E7   Gsus4 G Fsus4 F Cadd4   C

An - gie, _   where will it lead us from here? _____   1. With no

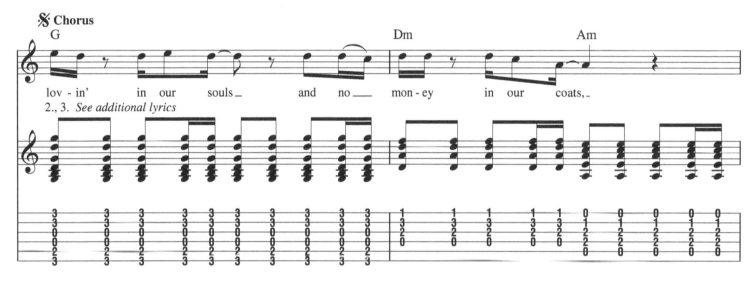

% **Chorus**
G   Dm   Am

lov - in'   in our souls _   and no _ mon - ey   in our coats, _
2., 3. *See additional lyrics*

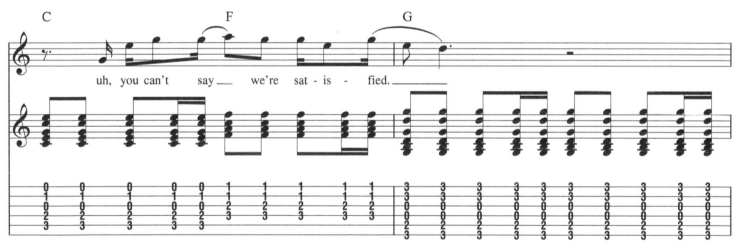

C   F   G

uh, you can't say _ we're sat - is - fied. _____

To Coda ⊕

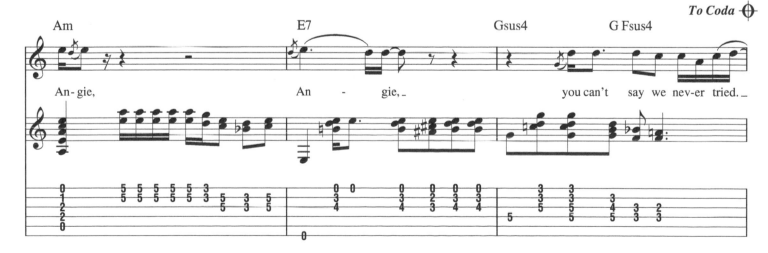

Am   E7   Gsus4   G Fsus4

An - gie,   An - gie, _   you can't say we nev-er tried. _

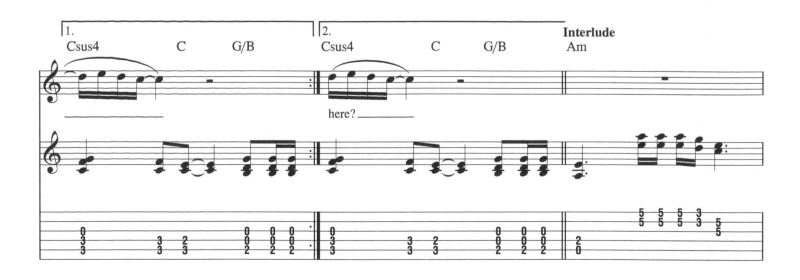

here?

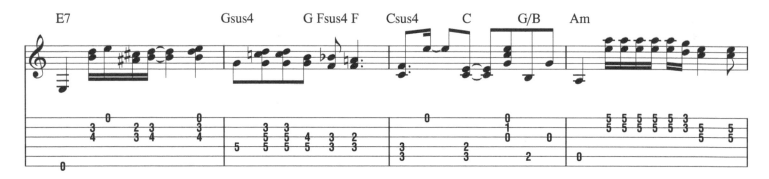

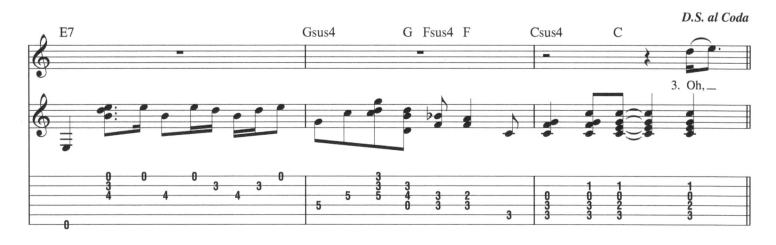

D.S. al Coda

3. Oh, ___

⊕ **Coda**

bye? _____ Yeah.

(An - gie,   An - gie,

4

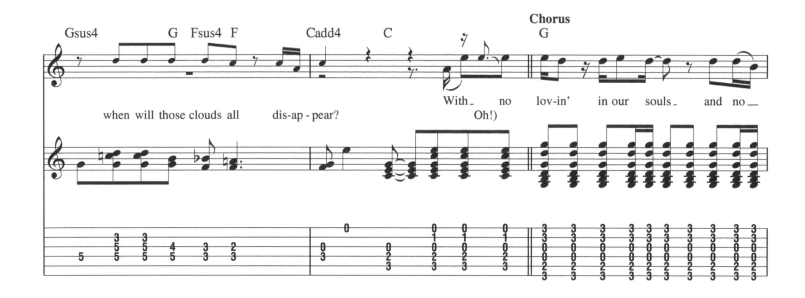

when will those clouds all dis-ap-pear? (Oh!) **Chorus** With_ no lov-in' in our souls_ and no_

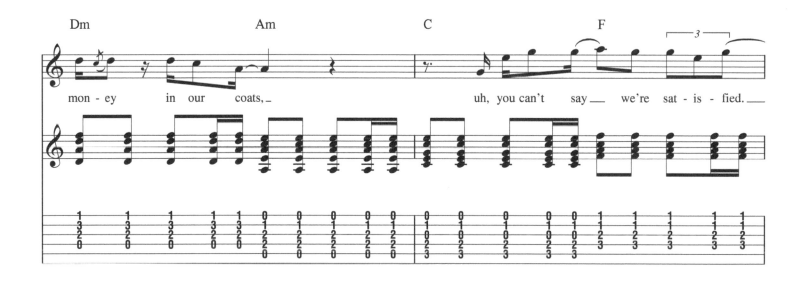

mon-ey in our coats,_ uh, you can't say_ we're sat-is-fied._

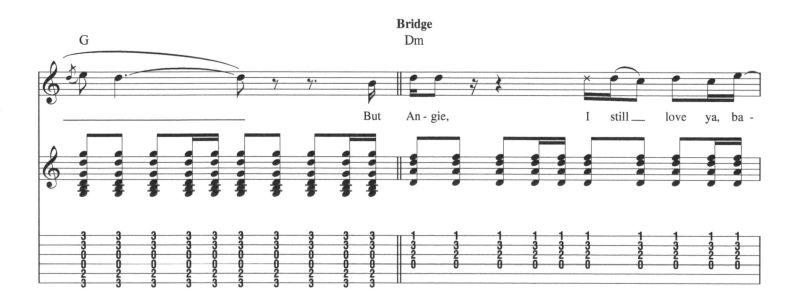

Bridge

But An-gie, I still_ love ya, ba-

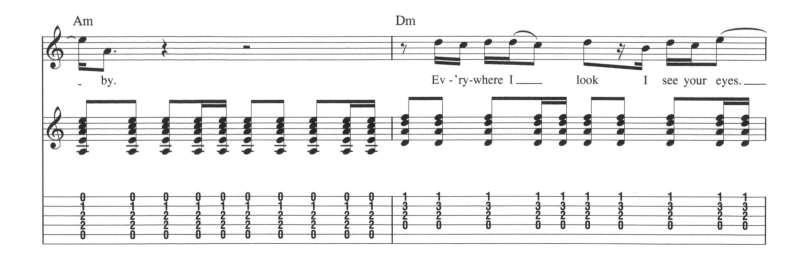

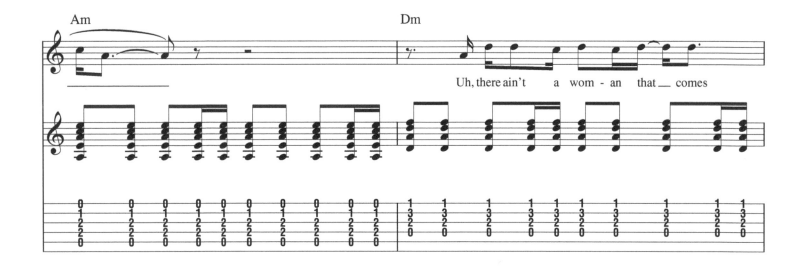

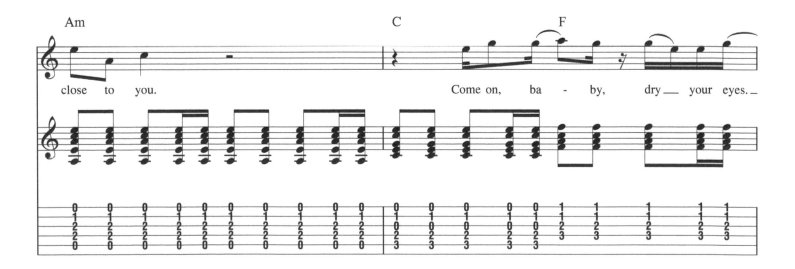

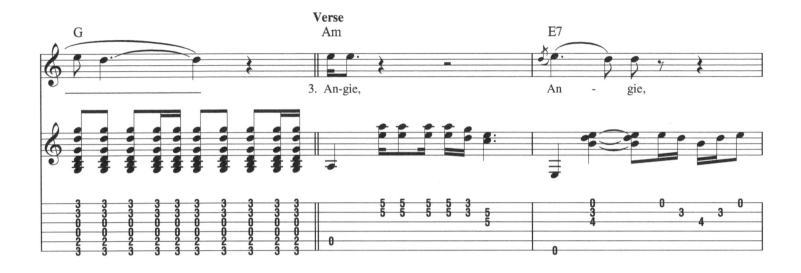

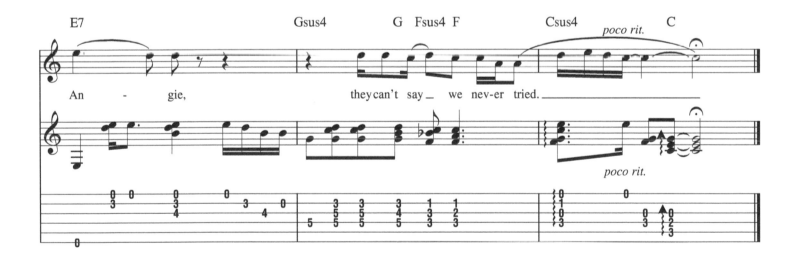

Additional Lyrics

2. A-Angie, you're beautiful, yes,
But ain't it time we said goodbye?
A-Angie, I still love ya.
Remember all those nights we cried?

Chorus 2. All the dreams we held so close
Seemed to all go up in smoke.
Uh, let me whisper in your ear.
Whispered: Angie, Angie,
Where will it lead us from here?

Chorus 3. Oh, Angie, don't you weep,
All your kisses still taste sweet.
I hate that sadness in your eyes.
But Angie, Angie,
A-ain't it time we said goodbye?

7

Behind Blue Eyes

Words and Music by Pete Townshend

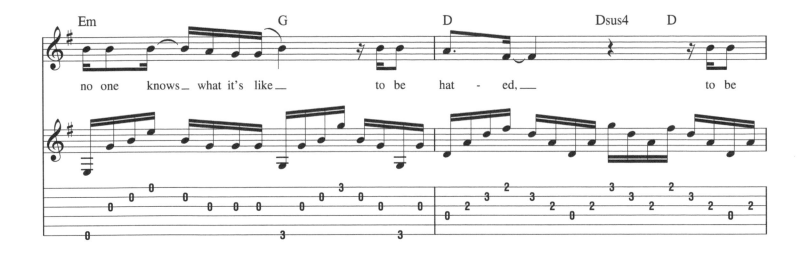

no one knows_ what it's like _ to be hat - ed, _ to be

fat - ed _ to tell - ing on - ly lies. But my

Chorus

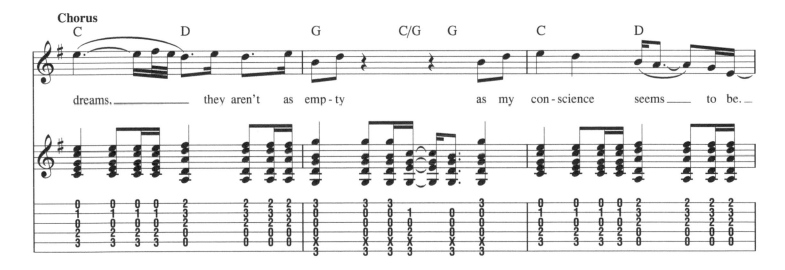

dreams, ____ they aren't as emp - ty as my con - science seems _ to be. _

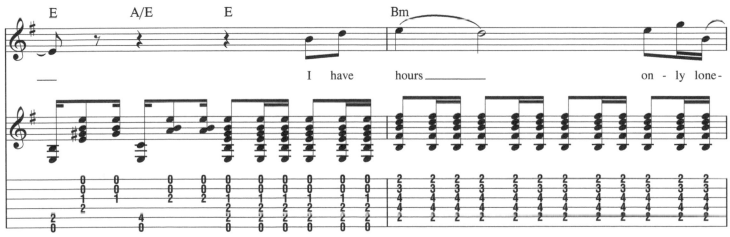

I have hours ____ on - ly lone-

9

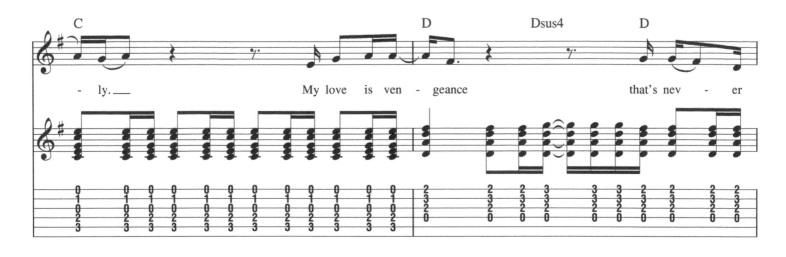

-ly.____ My love is ven - geance that's nev - er

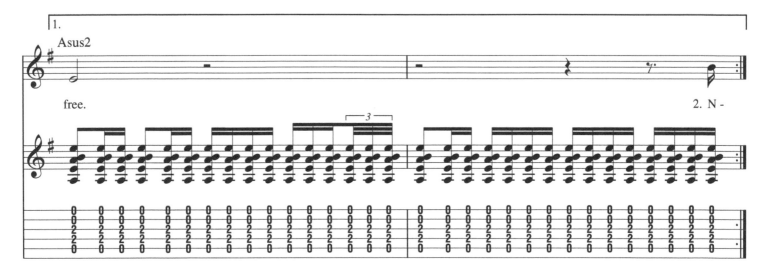

free. 2. N -

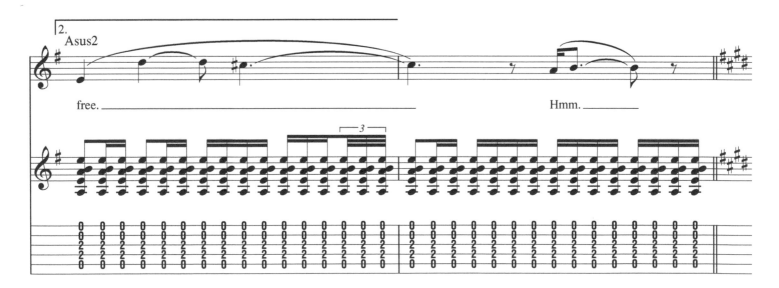

free.____ Hmm.____

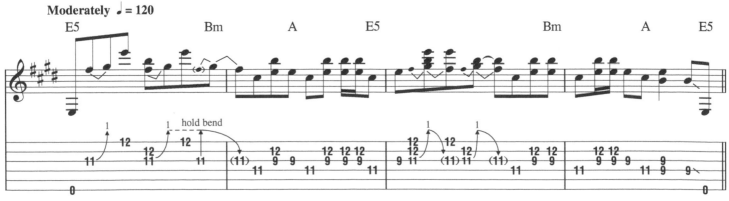

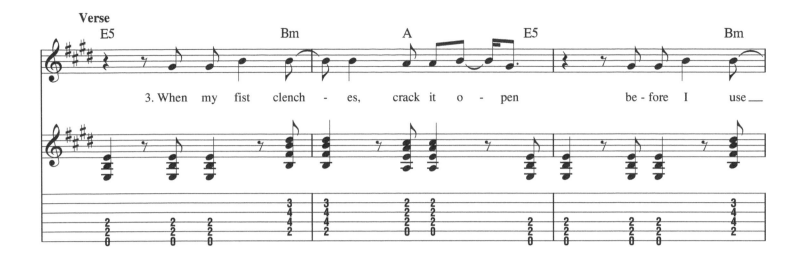

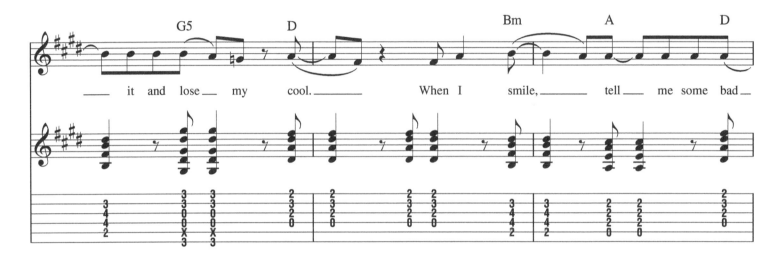

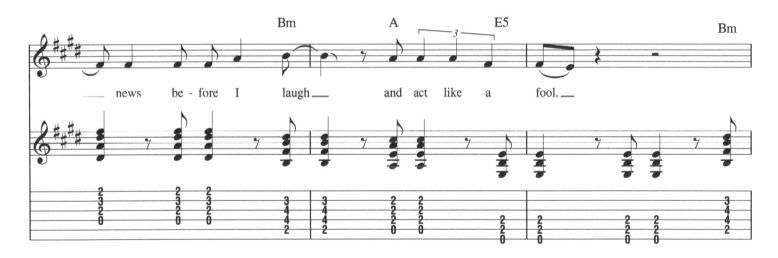

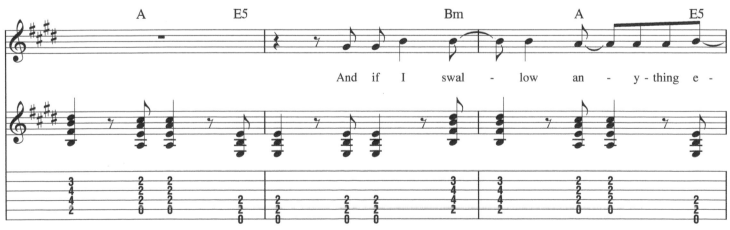

-vil, put your fin - ger down ___ my throat. And if I shiv-

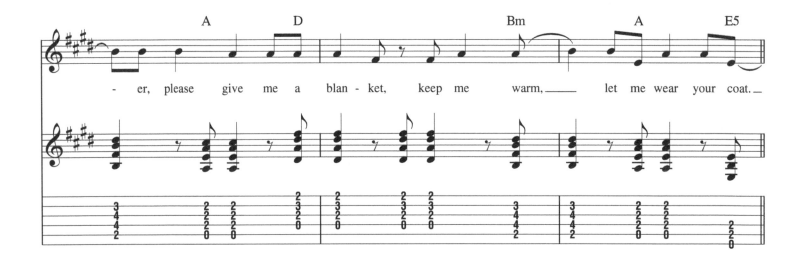

-er, please give me a blan - ket, keep me warm, ___ let me wear your coat. ___

Interlude

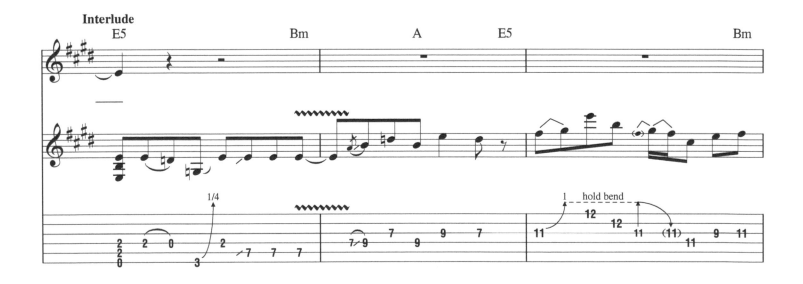

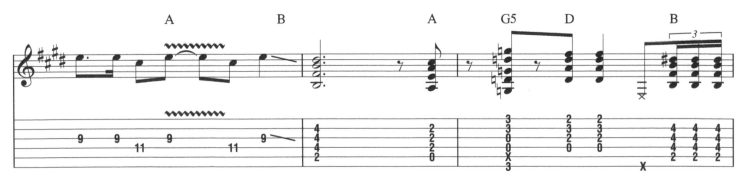

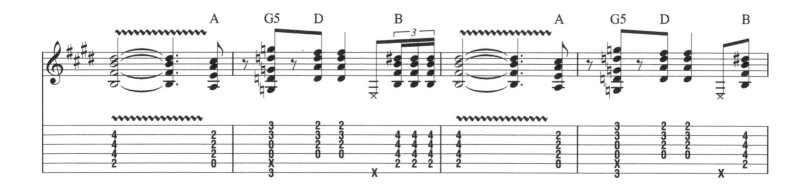

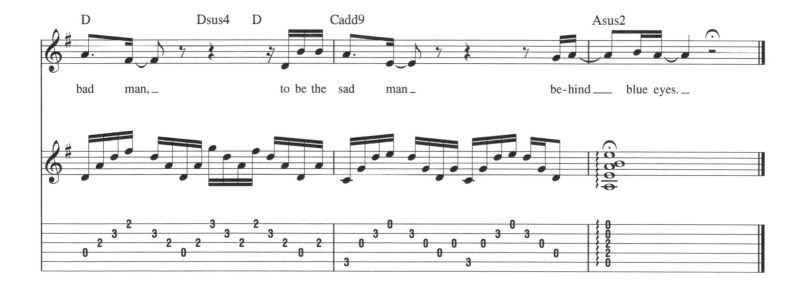

Additional Lyrics

2. N-no one knows what it's like to feel these feelings
   Like I do, and I blame you.
   N-no one bites back as hard on their anger,
   None of my pain and woe can show through.

Best of My Love

Words and Music by John David Souther, Don Henley and Glenn Frey

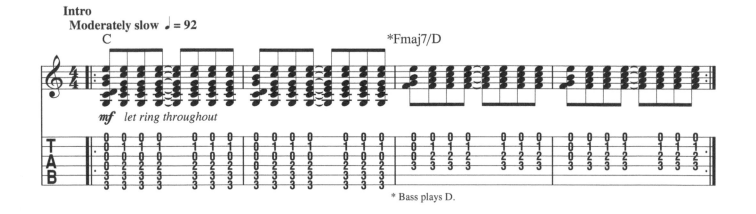

* Bass plays D.

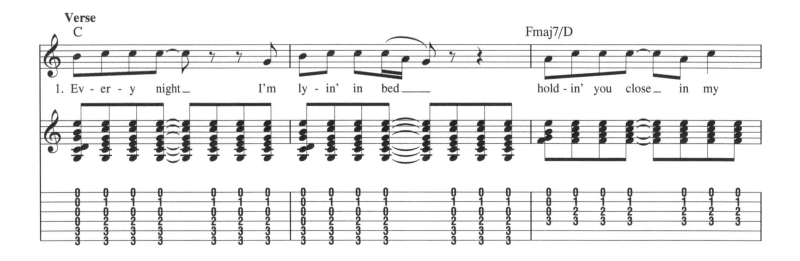

1. Ev-er-y night ___ I'm ly-in' in bed ___ hold-in' you close ___ in my

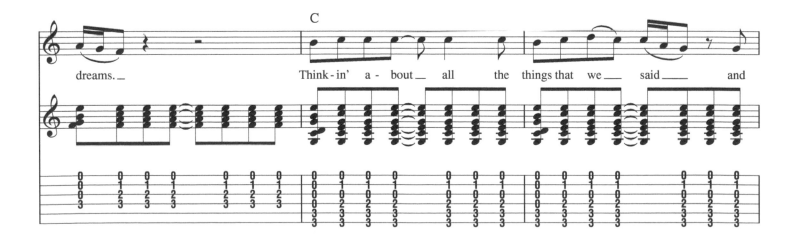

dreams. ___ Think-in' a-bout ___ all the things that we ___ said ___ and

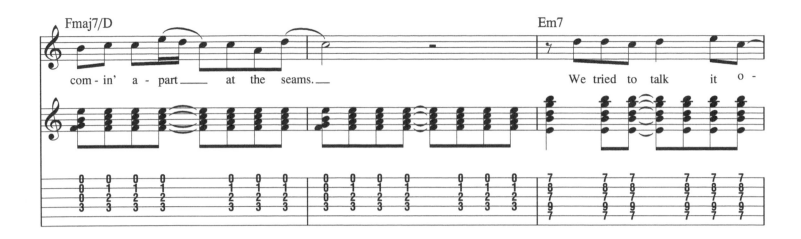

com-in' a-part ___ at the seams. ___   We tried to talk it o-

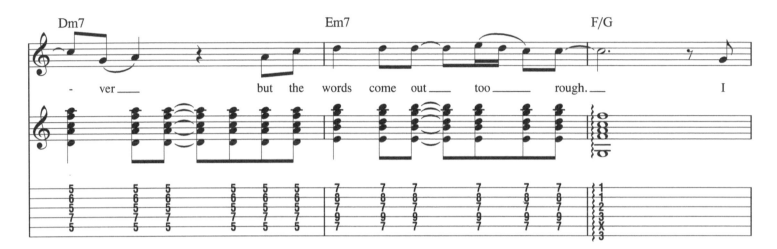

-ver ___ but the words come out ___ too ___ rough. ___   I

know you were try - in' to give me the best ___ of your ___ love.

$\mathcal{S}$ **Verse**

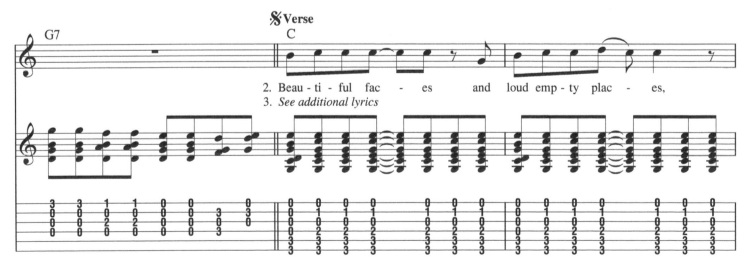

2. Beau - ti - ful fac - es   and loud emp - ty plac - es,

3. *See additional lyrics*

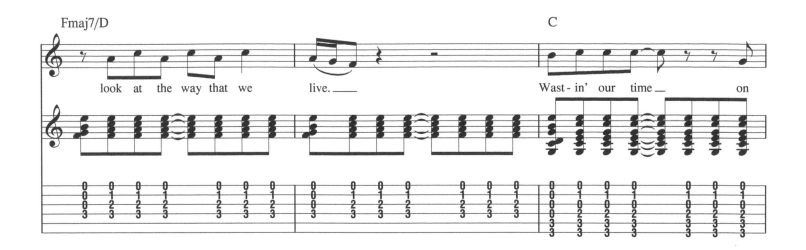

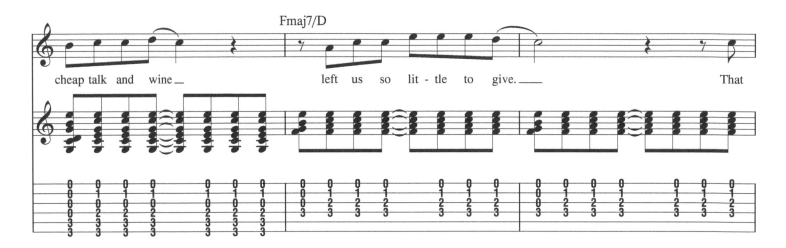

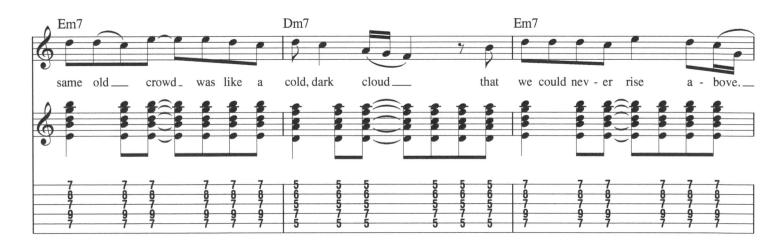

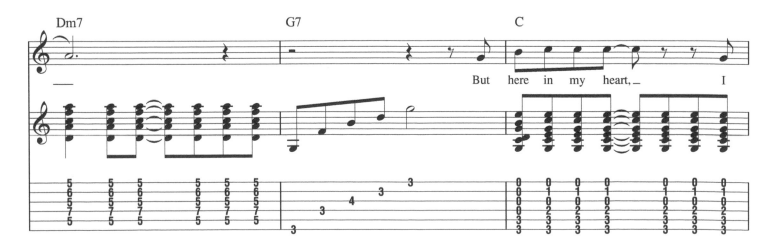

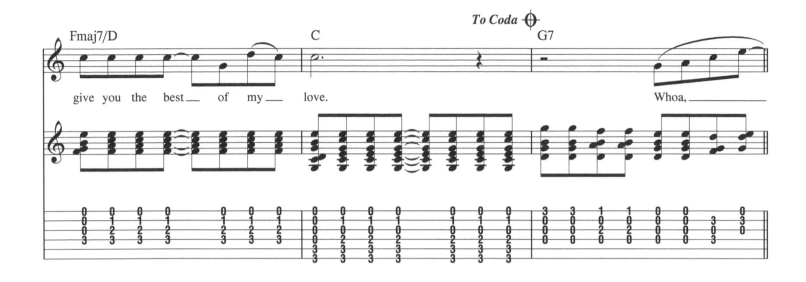

give you the best___ of my___ love.   Whoa,_____

sweet dar - lin',   you get the best of my
(You get the best of my___ love.)

love.___   Whoa,_____   sweet dar - lin',
                                                (You get the best of my love.)___

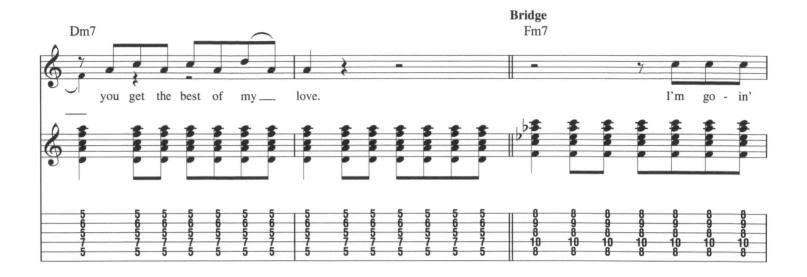

you get the best of my ___ love.

Bridge

I'm go - in'

back in time ___ and it's a sweet _____ dream. ___

It was a

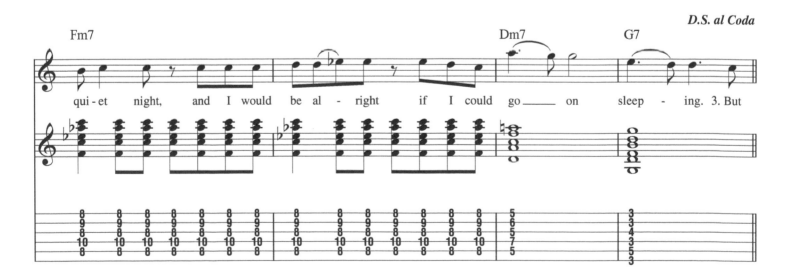

D.S. al Coda

qui - et night, and I would be al - right if I could go ___ on sleep - ing. 3. But

Coda

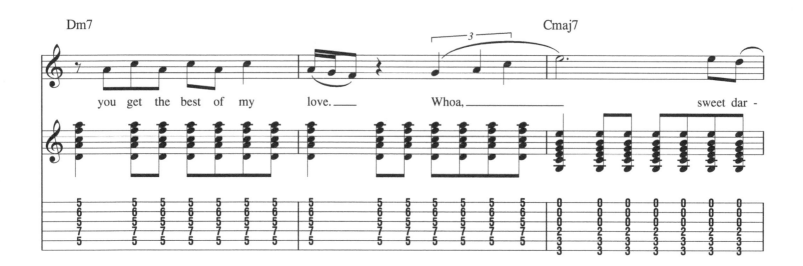

Additional Lyrics

3. But ev'ry morning I wake up and worry
   What's gonna happen today.
   You see it your way and I'll see it mine,
   But we both see it slippin' away.
   You know we always had each other, baby.
   I guess that wasn't enough.
   Oh, oh, but here in my heart,
   I give you the best of my love.

Blackbird

Words and Music by John Lennon and Paul McCartney

*Strum upstemmed notes w/ index finger of pick hand
whenever more than one upstemmed note appears.

1., 2., 3. Black-bird sing-ing in the dead of night,

{ 1., 3. take __ these bro-ken wings __ and learn __ to fly. __ }
{ 2. take __ these sunk-en eyes __ and learn __ to see. __ }

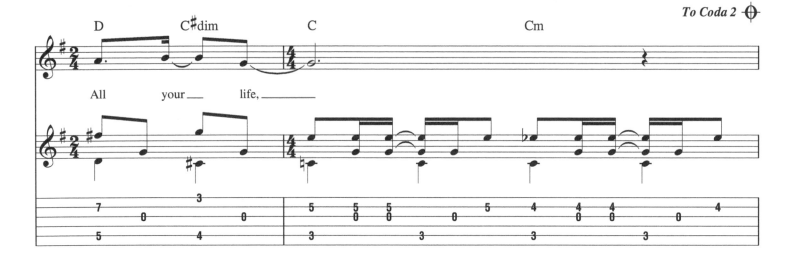

All your___ life,_____

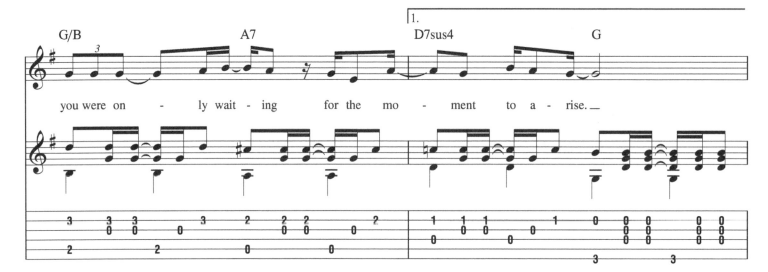

you were on - ly wait - ing for the mo - ment to a - rise.___

2.

𝄋 Bridge

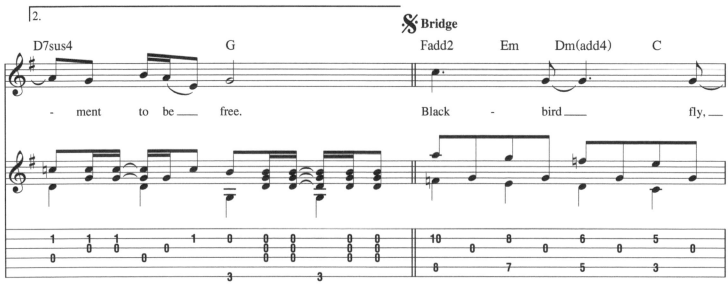

- ment to be___ free.   Black - bird___   fly,___

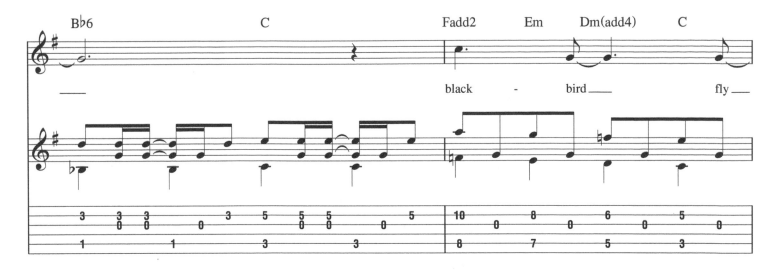

black - bird____ fly____

To Coda 1 ⊕

in - to the light____ of the dark black____

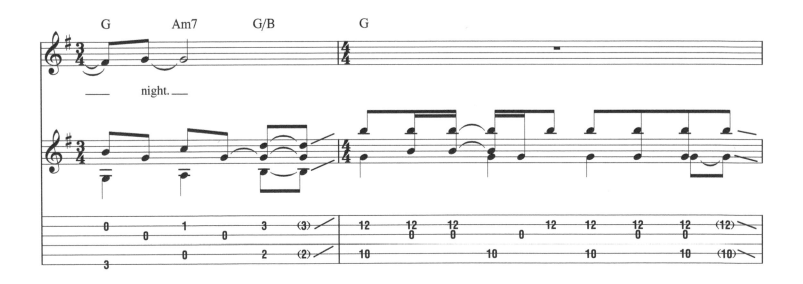

night.____

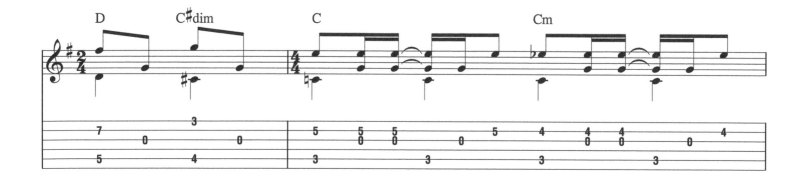

D.S. al Coda 1

Coda 1

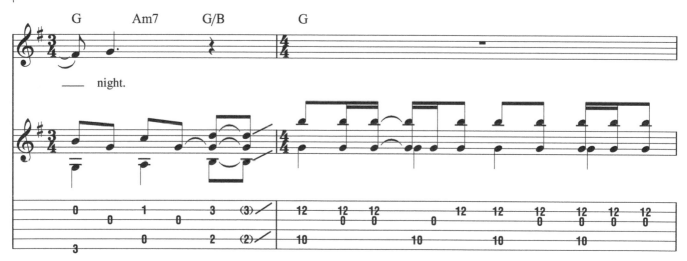

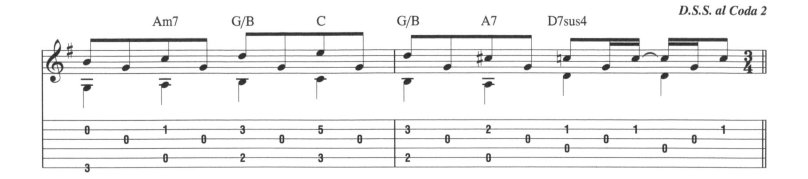

⊕Coda 2

you were on - ly wait-ing for this mo - ment to a - rise._

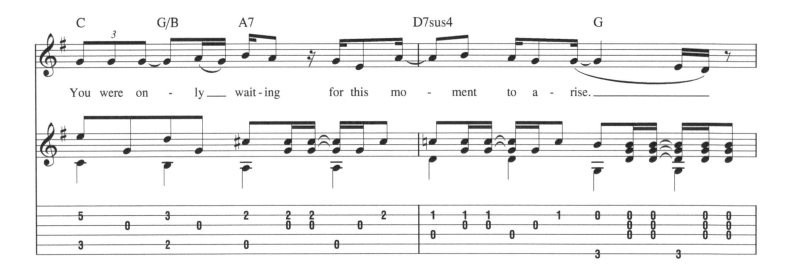

You were on - ly _ wait-ing for this mo - ment to a - rise._____

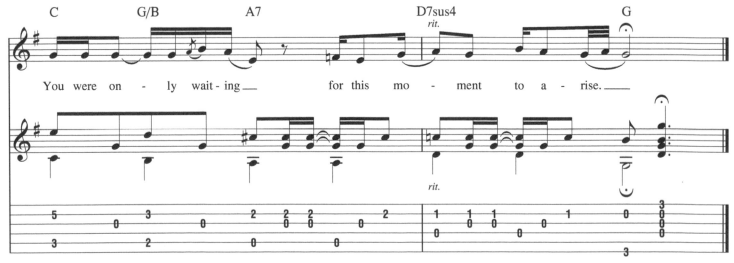

You were on - ly wait-ing ___ for this mo - ment to a - rise._

Dust in the Wind

Words and Music by Kerry Livgren

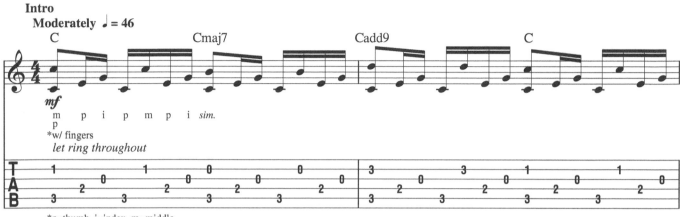

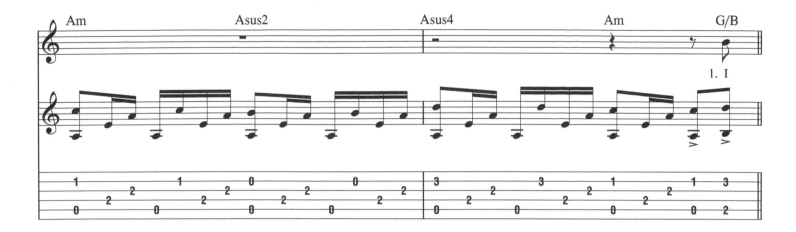

Verse

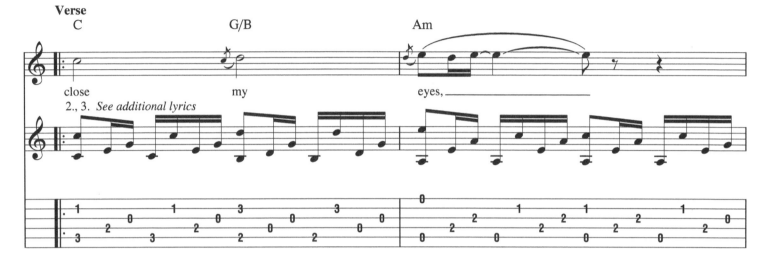

close my eyes,

2., 3. See additional lyrics

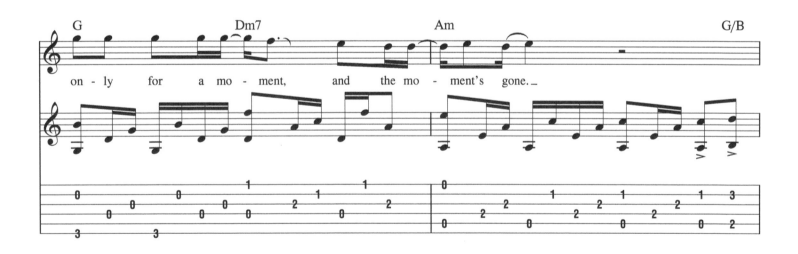

on - ly for a mo - ment, and the mo - ment's gone.

All my dreams

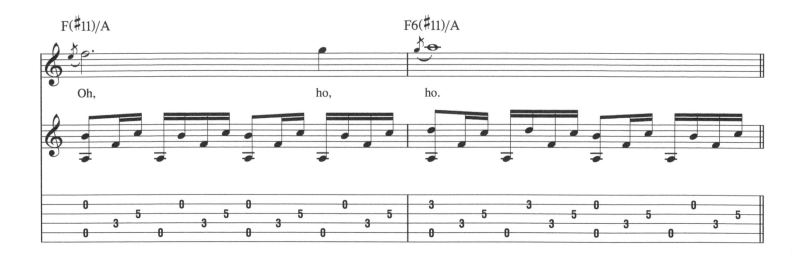

Oh, ho, ho.

Interlude

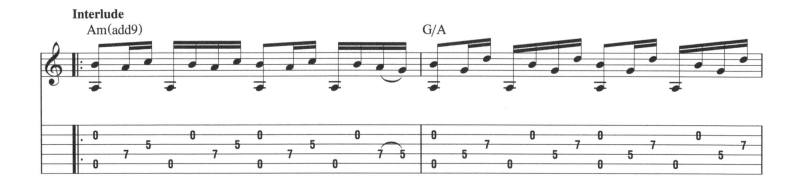

2nd time, D.C. al Coda

Coda

All we are __ is dust in __ the wind. __

(All we are __ is dust in __ the

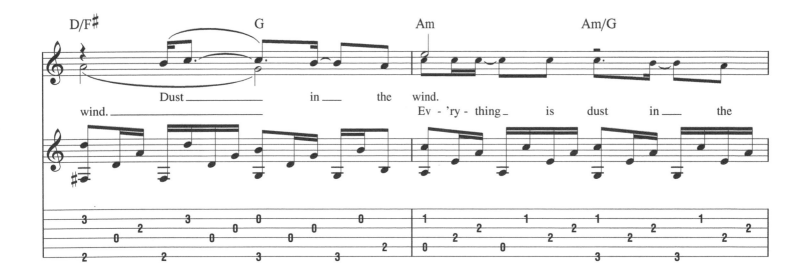

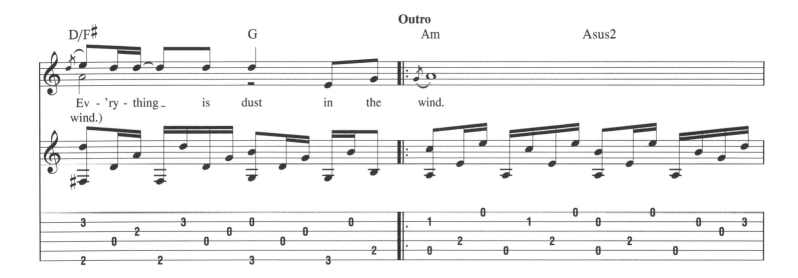

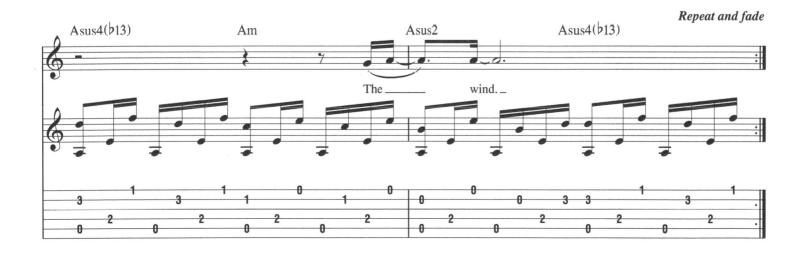

Additional Lyrics

2. Same old song.
   Just a drop of water in an endless sea.
   All we do
   Crumbles to the ground though we refuse to see.

3. Now don't hang on,
   Nothing lasts forever but the earth and sky.
   It slips away
   And all your money won't another minute buy.

Layla

Words and Music by Eric Clapton and Jim Gordon

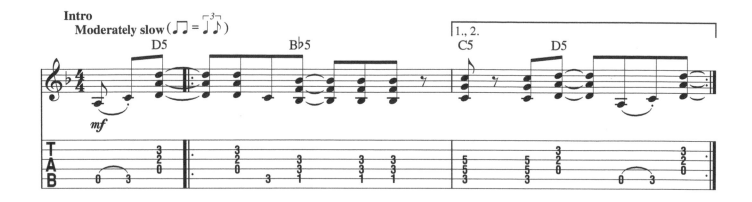

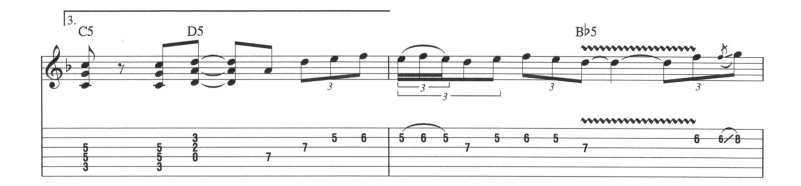

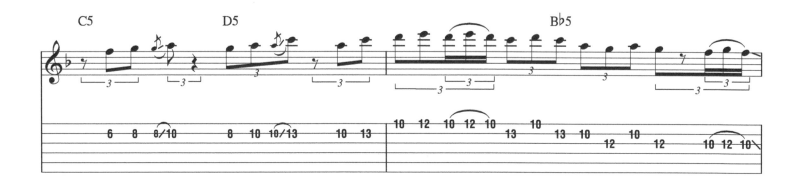

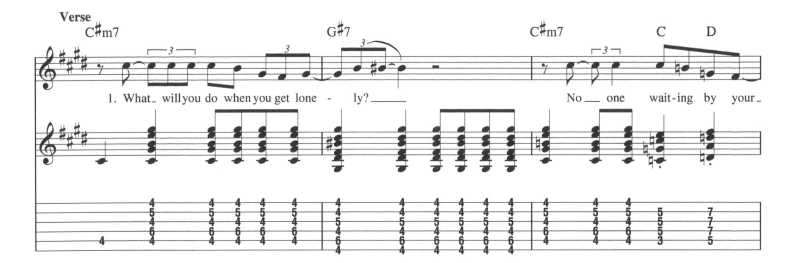

Verse

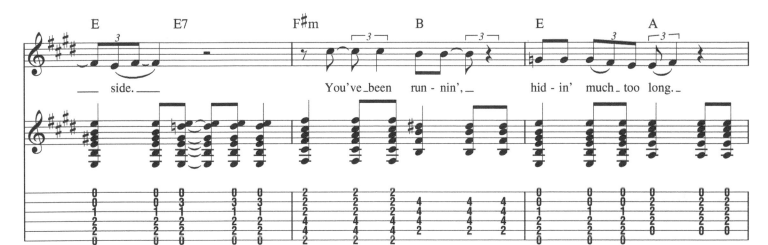

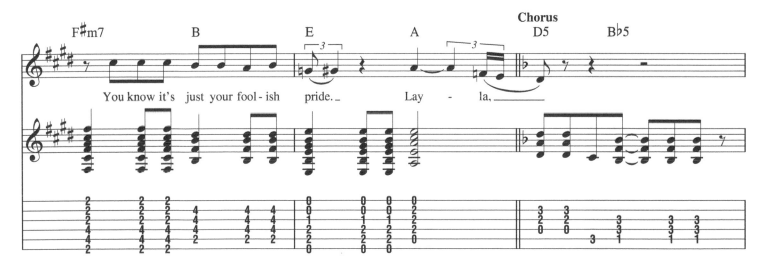

Chorus

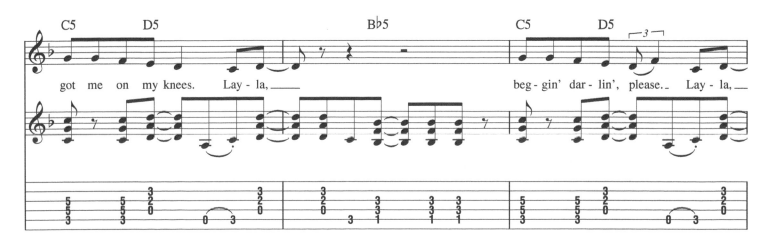

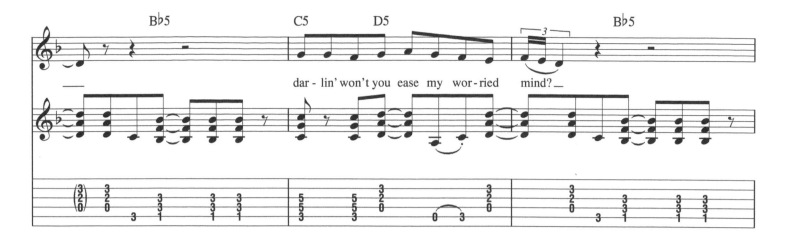

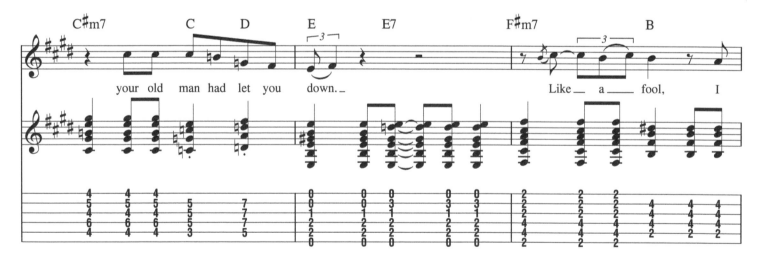

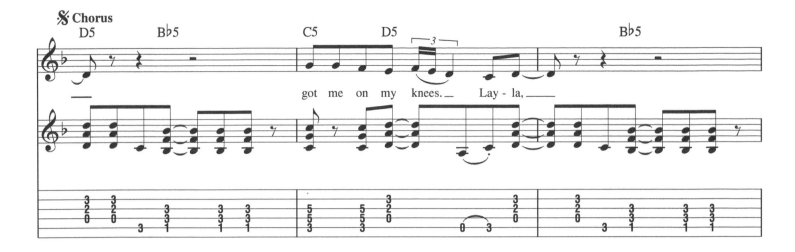

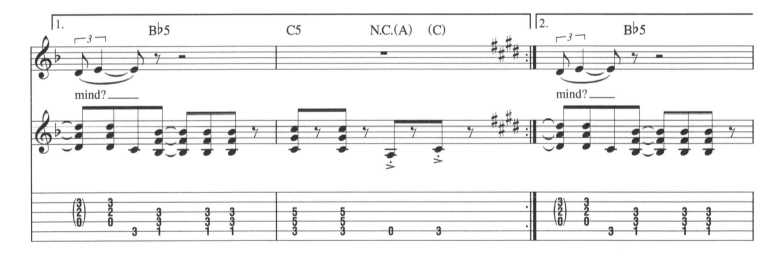

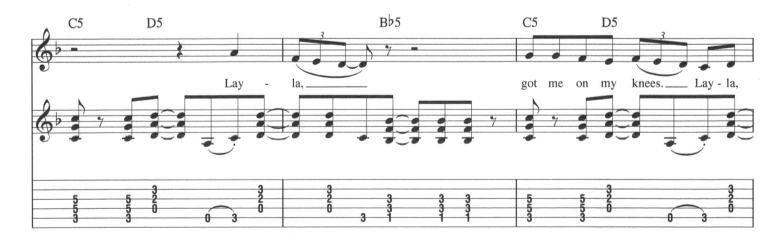

beg-gin' dar-lin', please.   Lay - la, _____

dar-lin', won't you ease my wor-ried mind?

Guitar Solo

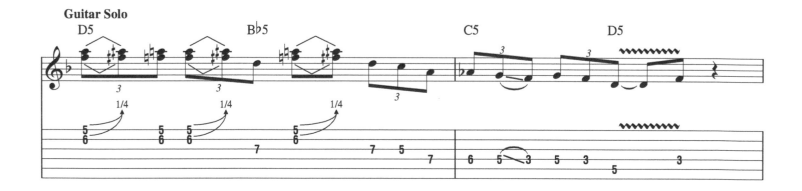

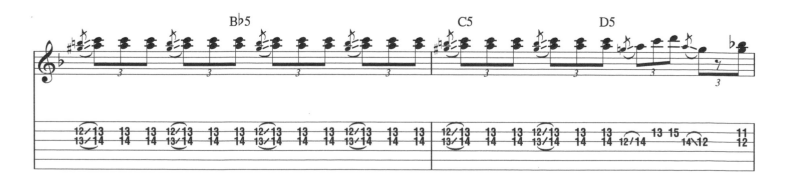

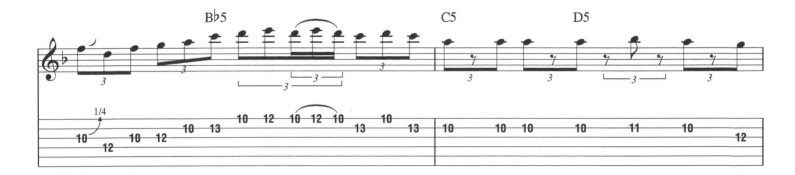

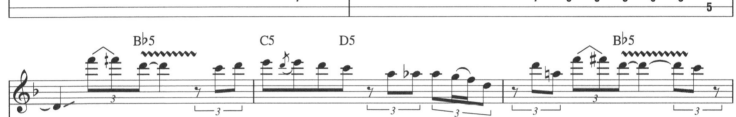

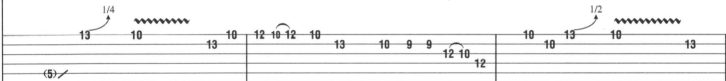

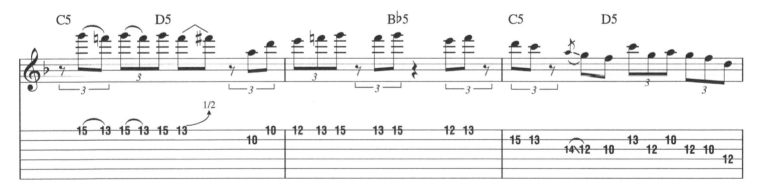

D.S. al Coda

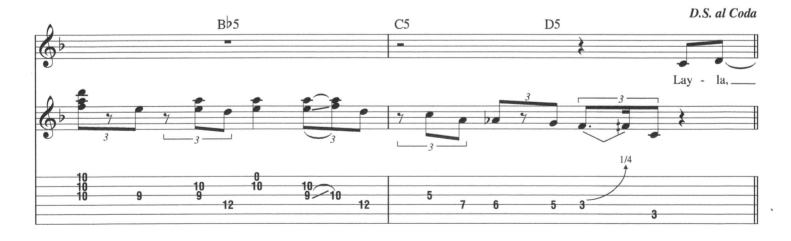

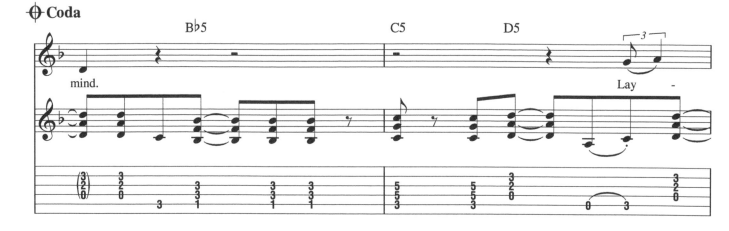

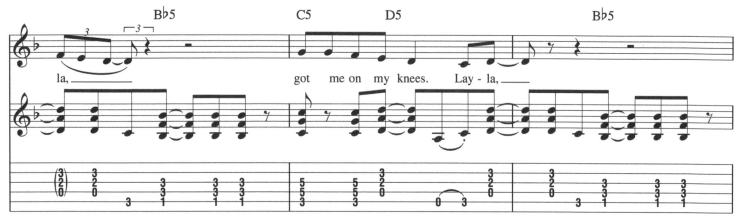

Additional Lyrics

2. Make the best of the situation,
   Before I fin'ly go insane.
   Please don't say we'll never find a way.
   Tell me all my love's in vain.

Night Moves

Words and Music by Bob Seger

Capo I

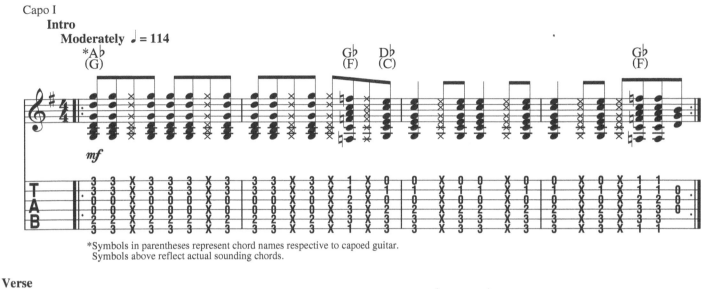

*Symbols in parentheses represent chord names respective to capoed guitar.
Symbols above reflect actual sounding chords.

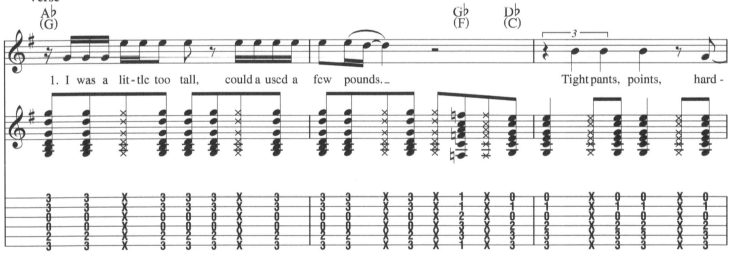

1. I was a lit-tle too tall, could a used a few pounds. _____ Tight pants, points, hard-

- ly re - nown. _____ She was a black- haired beau-ty with big, dark eyes, _____

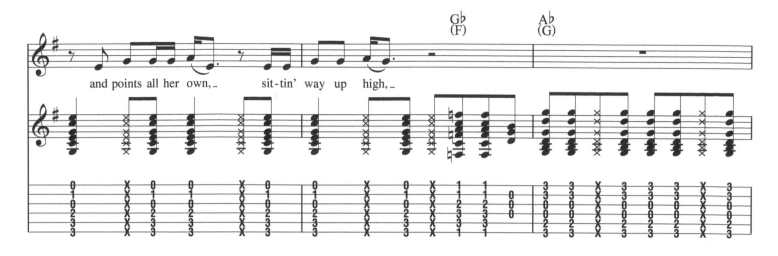

and points all her own,__ sit-tin' way up high,__

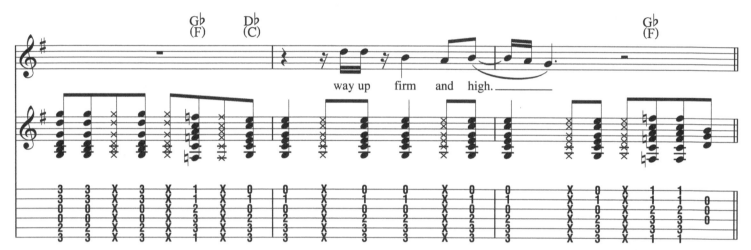

way up firm and high._____

Verse

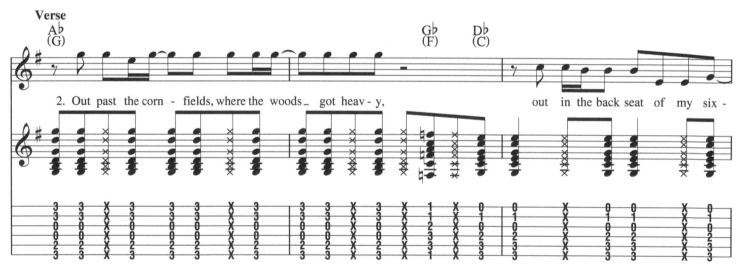

2. Out past the corn - fields, where the woods__ got heav - y,   out in the back seat of my six -

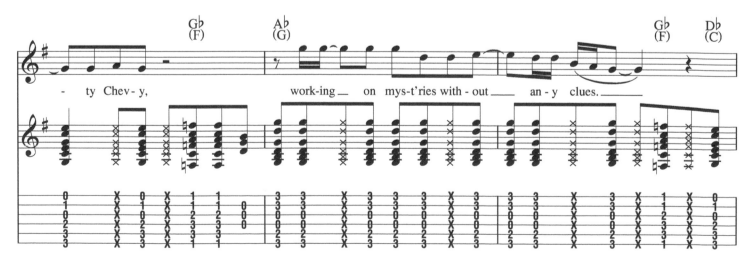

- ty Chev - y,   work-ing__ on mys-t'ries with - out____ an - y clues._____

%‌ **Chorus**

Work-in' on our night moves, _____
See additional lyrics

try'n' to make some

front page, drive-in news. _____ Work-in' on our night moves,

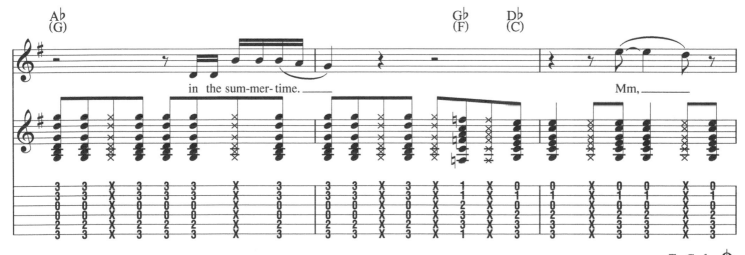

in the sum-mer-time. _____ Mm, _____

To Coda ⊕

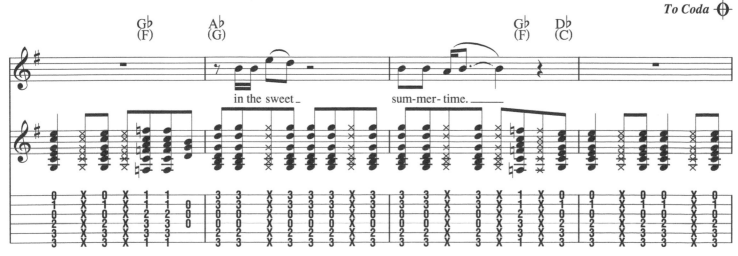

in the sweet _ sum-mer-time. _____

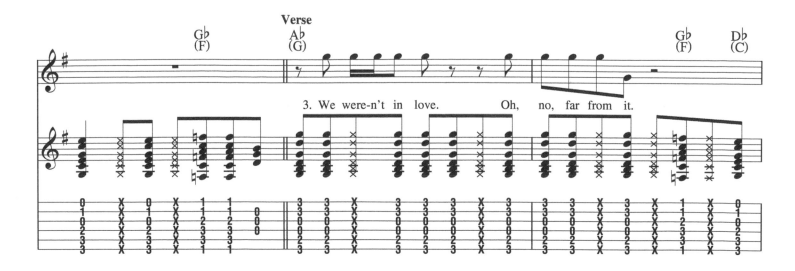

3. We were-n't in love. Oh, no, far from it.

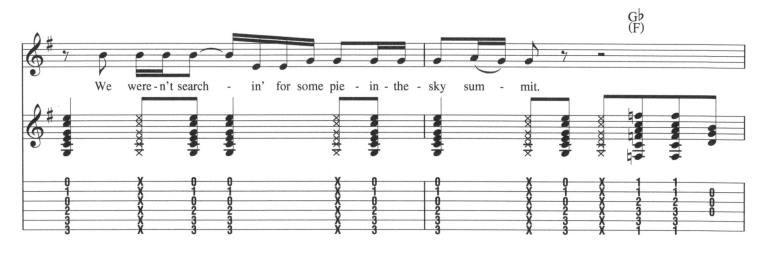

We were-n't search — in' for some pie - in-the - sky sum — mit.

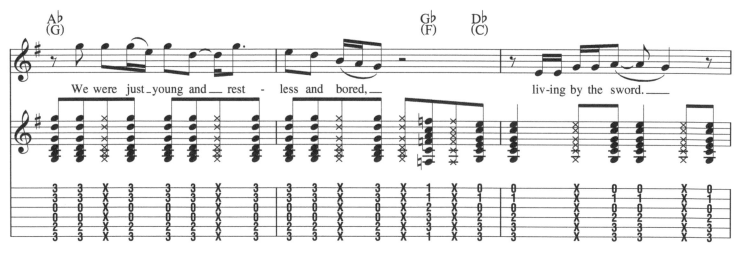

We were just young and rest - less and bored, liv-ing by the sword.

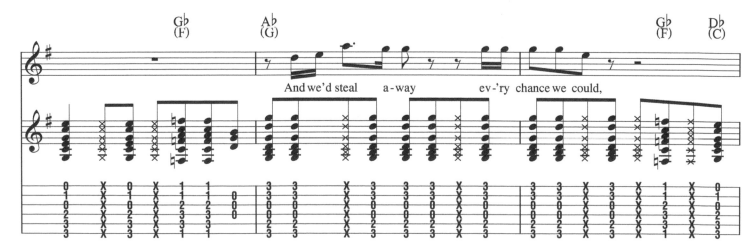

And we'd steal a - way ev-'ry chance we could,

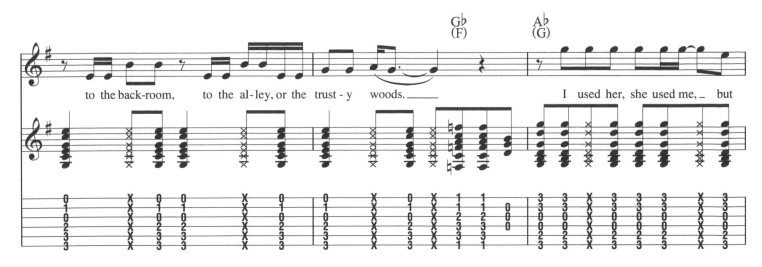

D.S. al Coda

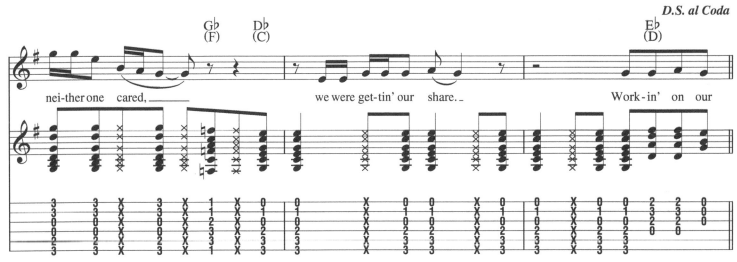

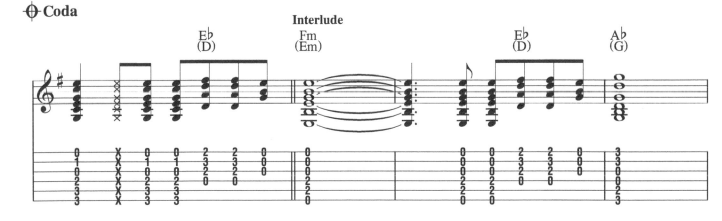

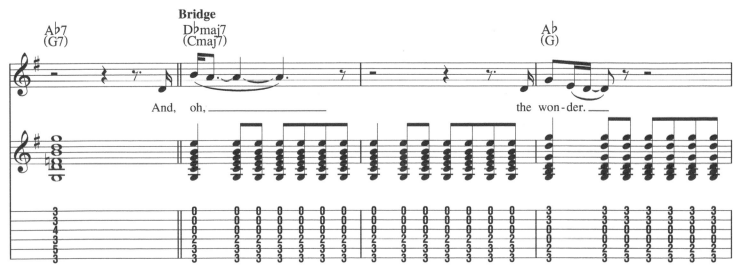

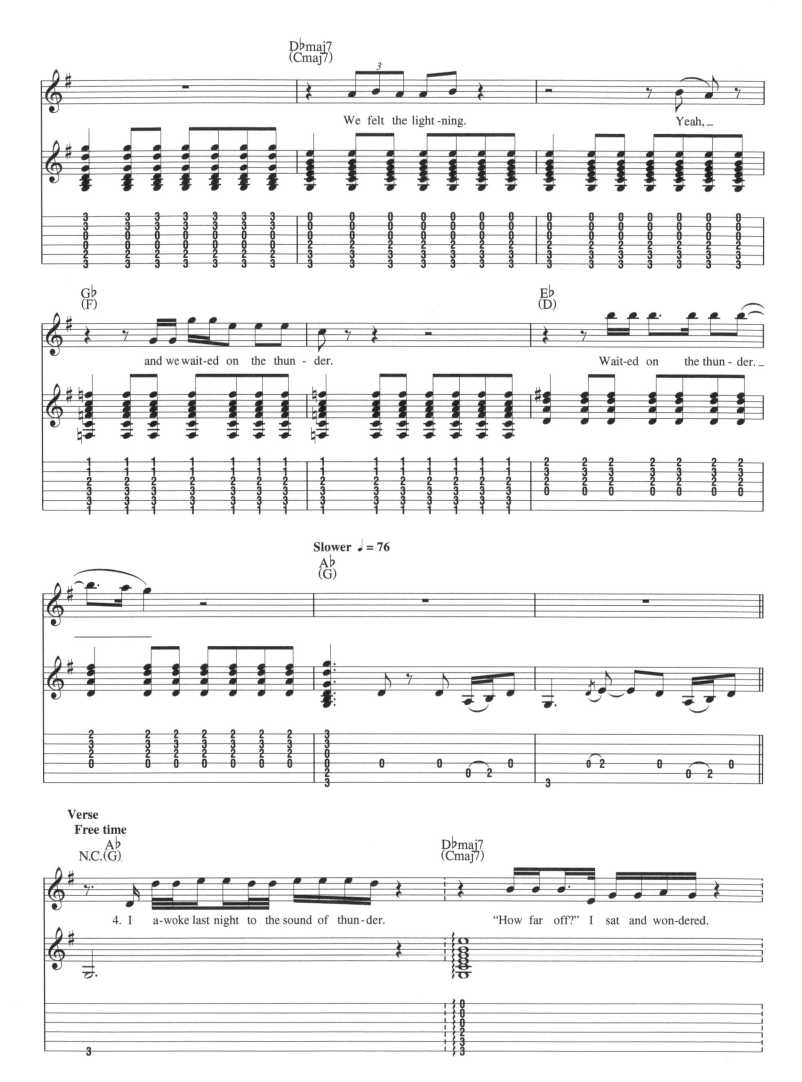

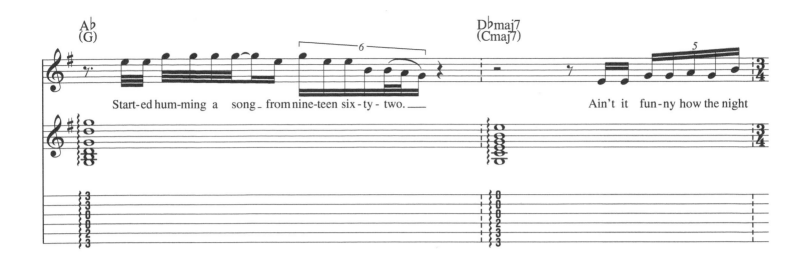

Start-ed hum-ming a song from nine-teen six-ty-two. Ain't it fun-ny how the night

moves? When you just don't seem to have as much to lose.

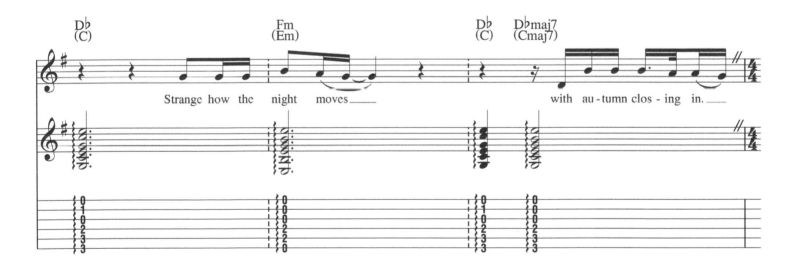

Strange how the night moves with au-tumn clos-ing in.

Moderately ♩ = 114

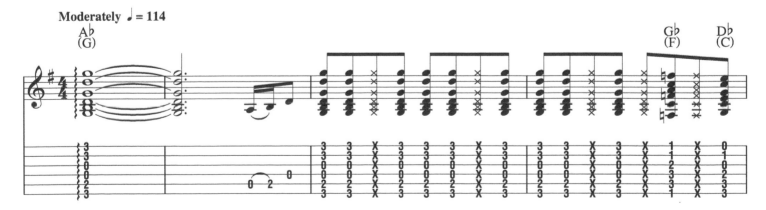

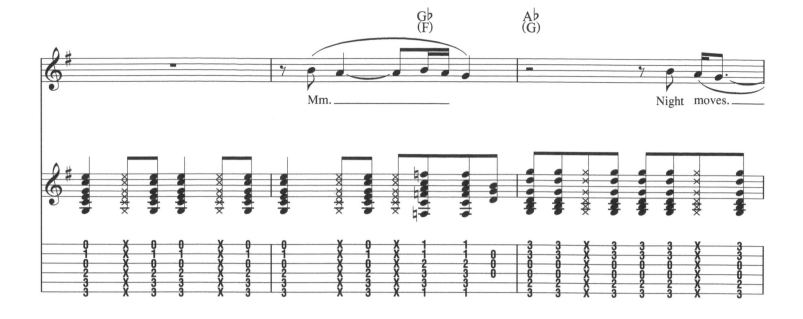

Mm.   Night   moves.

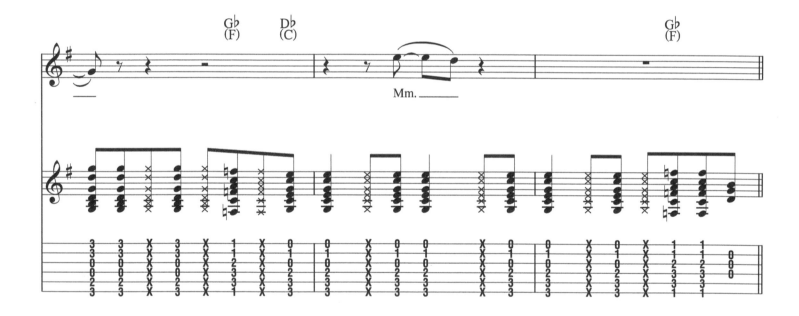

Mm.

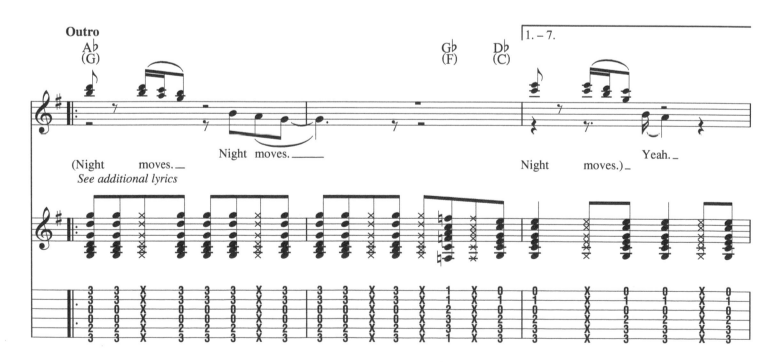

(Night   moves.)

See additional lyrics

Night   moves.   Night   moves.)   Yeah.

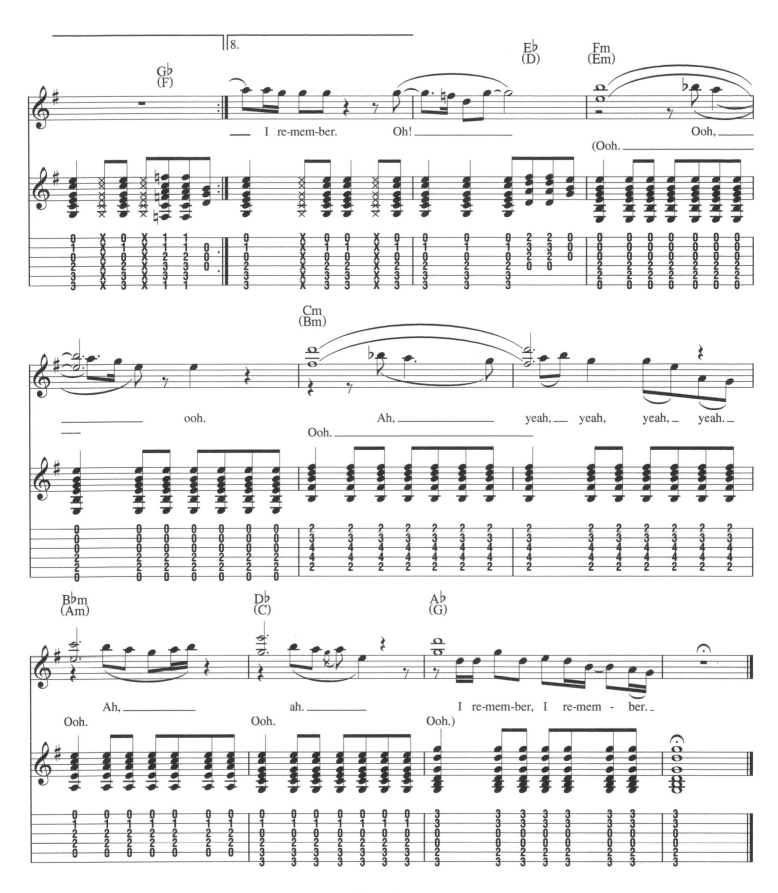

Additional Lyrics

Chorus Workin' on our night moves,
Tryin' to lose the awkward teenage blues.
Workin' on our night moves, mm,
And it was summertime, mm,
Sweet summertime, summertime.

Outro Moves, I sure remember the night moves.
In the morning, I remember.
Funny how you remember.
I remember, I remember, I remember, I remember.
Oh, oh, oh.
Keep it workin', workin' and practicin'.
Workin' and practicin' all of the night moves.
Night moves. Oh.
I remember, yeah, yeah, yeah, I remember.
Ooh. I remember, Lord, I remember, Lord, I remember.

Yesterday

Words and Music by John Lennon and Paul McCartney

Tune down 1 step:
(low to high) D-G-C-F-A-D

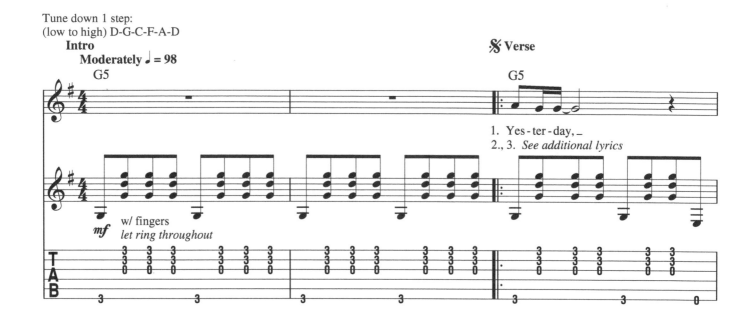

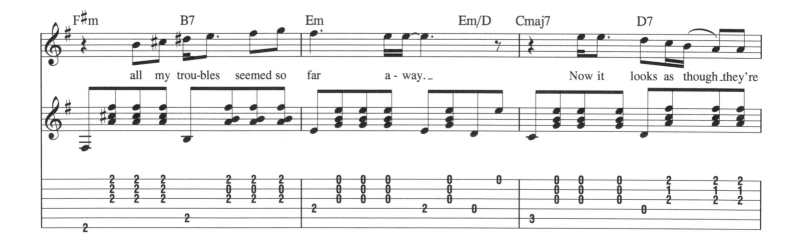

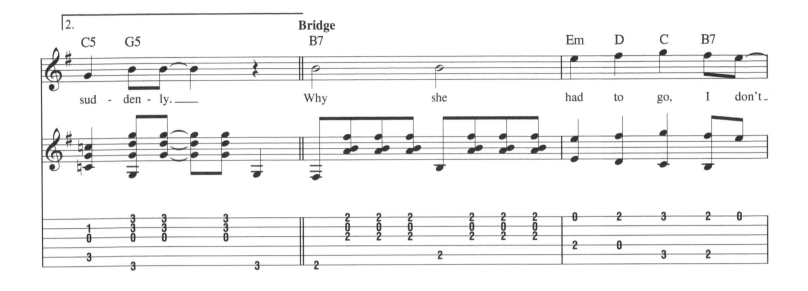

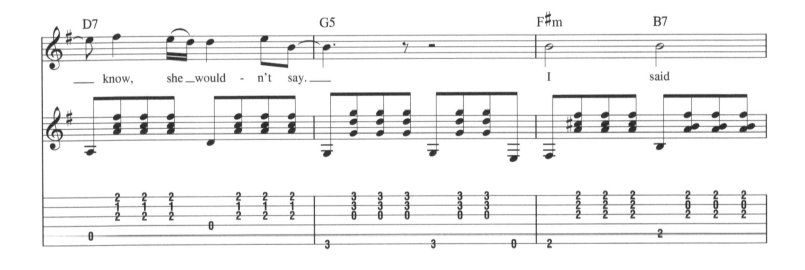

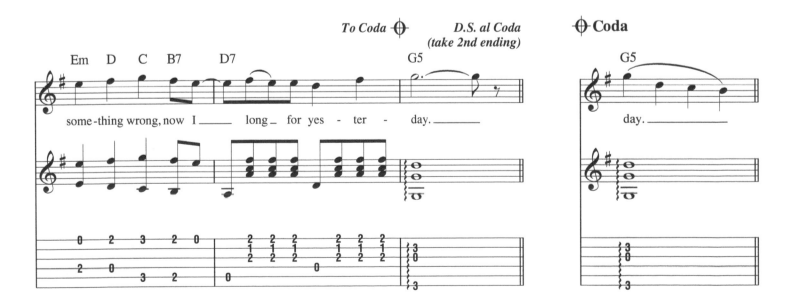

Verse

4. Yes-ter day,␣ love was such an eas-y game to play.␣

Now I need␣ a place␣ to hide a-way.␣ Oh, I be-lieve␣ in

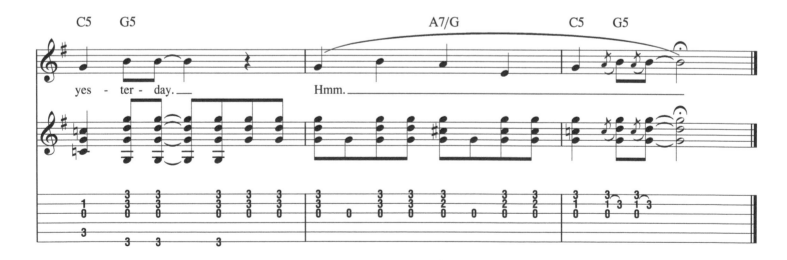

yes-ter-day.␣ Hmm.␣

Additional Lyrics

2. Suddenly, I'm not half the man I used to be.
   There's a shadow hanging over me.
   Oh, yesterday came suddenly.

3. Yesterday, love was such an easy game to play.
   Now I need a place to hide away.
   Oh, I believe in yesterday.